# the White Robed Monk

## BOOKS BY IRA PROGOFF

At A Journal Workshop: The Basic Text and Guide for Using the Intensive Journal Process, 1975

The Symbolic and the Real, 1963

Depth Psychology and Modern Man, 1959

The Death and Rebirth of Psychology, 1956

The Cloud of Unknowing, 1957

The Image of an Oracle, 1964

Jung's Psychology and Its Social Meaning, 1953

Jung, Synchronicity and Human Destiny, 1973

The Star/Cross, 1971

The White Robed Monk, 1972

The Well and The Cathedral, 1971, 1977

*With an essay on its use in Process Meditation*

Ira Progoff

SECOND, REVISED EDITION

*DIALOGUE HOUSE LIBRARY / NEW YORK*

Published by Dialogue House Library
80 East 11 Street, New York, New York 10003

First Printing, 1972
Second Printing, 1976
Second Enlarged Edition, 1979


Printed in the United States of America

*Library of Congress Cataloging in Publication Data*

Progoff, Ira

1. Meditations I *The White Robed Monk*

PS3566.R65W5 1979 811'.5'4 79-1553
ISBN 0-87941-007-8

# *Table of Contents*

INTRODUCTION
TO THE SECOND, REVISED EDITION

# *The White Robed Monk as an Entrance to Process Meditation*

*The White Robed Monk* is one of a series of *entrance meditations* that have evolved out of experience and practice with the *Intensive Journal* process. They are *entrance meditations* in the special sense that they open a path inward into the various dimensions and levels at the depth of our being. They are door openers and they take each of us through the entry way at the surface of consciousness. Once we are past the entrance to the house of our inner being, we are each free to explore and experience the varieties of awareness and belief that become possible when we enter the depth of the Self.

*Entrance meditations* do not prescribe in advance what we shall discover when we are moving about on the inner levels. They merely take us inward and give us entry. Then they leave us in freedom so that each of us can explore and discover as much of the infinities of truth as we can absorb; and so that each of us can find our new knowing and beliefs in the degrees and stages and aspects that are appropriate to our lives.

This is the ultimate religious freedom toward which we aspire: the ability to move in freedom through the vastness of spiritual space so that we can find ever more of the infinities of truth to experience by ourselves as individuals and to share with our fellow humans. Of course we require the freedom for each of us to reach and to espouse whatever particular beliefs and commitments seem valid to us as persons. That is religious freedom on the outer political level, but the greater religious freedom is on the spiritual level. It is the capacity to move and explore inwardly in freedom so as to make personal discoveries by direct experience at the profound levels of life. *Entrance meditations* seek to open the doorway to that freedom.

Two famous statements are indicative of the concept that underlies the work with entrance meditations. One is the profound phrase of St. Augustine in which he speaks of "the magnitude of the soul." He was calling attention to the fact that the spiritual dimension of life contains a vastness that we cannot anticipate before we enter it, and that it opens progressively to us as we explore it. Our entrance meditations undertake the practical task of providing a means of entering that magnitude and beginning the exploration.

The other important statement is the Biblical phrase, "In my father's house are many mansions." It is saying that within the dimension of spiritual reality, within the magnitude of the soul, there are many facets and aspects, a great diversity of awarenesses and knowings for us to reach. In entering the great depth of being it is important for us to be not merely within the house but also to visit its many rooms so that we can eventually make a choice as to which rooms we wish to remain in at length.

The goal of an entrance meditation is thus not only to enable us to gain entry to the house but also to enter the individual rooms. *The White Robed Monk* consists of a sequence of eight meditations that move progressively inward to deeper levels of being. Throughout there is an underlying unity of theme and experience, but in each of them there are special points of contact and awareness that may be opened. There are many of these along the unitary path of meditative experience, like the many rooms in the house, and each of us may remain as long in any of the rooms as feels right to us at the time. Thus we wish to give ourselves ample latitude in silence to honor and pursue our feelings, our curiosities and our intuitions, as we explore the inner dimension of being.

Let me say a few words about the background of these meditations, and then speak of the practical means of using *The White Robed Monk* as an aid to inner experience both privately and in groups.

In its present form *The White Robed Monk* is a sequence of meditations describing a series of experiences that came to me over a period of time culminating in 1971. The experiences themselves came a few at a time and, as they were described and amplified, they gradually evolved into a full unit of meditation. They seek to convey the quality of reality in a particular experience. But the purpose of these meditations is not primarily to communicate or to describe. It is to establish an atmosphere in which each person can reach within the terms of their own experience a level of depth in their perception of spiritual reality. *The White Robed Monk* meditations are offered as a way of entry to this depth, and it is in this sense that they are called *entrance meditations.* They are a means of entering into the place where we can each make our own contact with an aspect of spiritual reality by means of the symbols and images that come to us in the depth of our experience.

The development of these meditations has come in the course of their being used at the *Intensive Journal* workshops. I found that when I read segments of these meditations as part of the *Intensive Journal* work of inward focusing they were effective in establishing a quiet atmosphere to help people draw their lives into perspective. The readings provide an extra quality of depth in keeping with the goal of the *Intensive Journal* process of drawing forth meaning in each individual life. The practice of reading sections of *The White Robed Monk* at Journal Workshops has continued over the years, especially since many people have reported to me that it enables them to make contact with a more-than-personal source of understanding and renewal in their lives. It has been significant to find that this deepening of contact takes place whether their experience moves within the specific symbolism of *The White Robed Monk* or whether they simply draw upon the atmosphere that is set by the meditations so that they are stimulated to experience a free movement of symbolism and imagery of their own.

*The White Robed Monk* meditations were first published in 1972, and that edition increased their use as an adjunct to the *Intensive Journal* work. Although they were not distributed publicly but only as part of the *Intensive Journal* program, there was need for a reprinting in 1976. They have continued to be used in the workshops, and they have also been used by me in my private meditations, leading to a number of new awarenesses and extensions. Through the dialogue process of being shared by many at the workshops and of being reentered repeatedly in my own experiences, *The White Robed Monk* meditations have been expanded and have moved toward a fuller format with additional content and with a structure that makes possible more consistent and disciplined use.

This new edition incorporates these enlargements of the text. In addition, since it is now presented as a sequence of eight distinct meditations, *The White Robed Monk* lends itself to being used in workshops and in non-doctrinal religious services. Its primary purpose, however, is for deepening the quality of meditation carried through by individuals in their privacy. Even its use in workshops and religious services has this as its goal. The personal use of *The White Robed Monk* is most important, and in these introductory remarks I want to discuss the main practical factors that are involved in it.

In the larger framework of Process Meditation of which *The White Robed Monk* is a particular aspect, there is a cycle of experience that plays a fundamental role. It is the cycle of movement from the activity of outer life proceeding into a condition of stillness. At the depth of that stillness, new ideas, images and awarenesses are activated, and as these come to the fore of consciousness they lead to a new round of activity both on the outer and inner levels of our life. We go from active to passive to active again, in a continuous, self-renewing movement that encompasses both the contemplative inner side of our life and the worldly outer expressions.

This conception of the continuous cycle of life experience derives from the broad view of the quest for spiritual meaning that is fundamental to the philosophy of Process Meditation.* In its perspective, human experience unfolds as a unity, the outer and the inner phases of life being but two sides of a single coin. Another way to say it is that they are the systole and diastole of a single process. What takes place in one has its consequences in the other, each responding to the other and bringing about new experiences and awarenesses as the process continues.

In the perspective of Process Meditation our religious life cannot be separated from the context of our life as a whole. It is the totality of our experiences that lead to spiritual awareness, the activities of our outer life in interrelationship with the emotions and thoughts of our inner life. One of the primary tasks of any method of meditation is to draw these opposites into harmony with each other, at least to draw them into a relationship that is in sufficient balance to make possible further productive happenings.

A clear example of this occurs in the sequence of entrance meditations that is a companion volume to *The White Robed Monk.* In *The Well and*

* See Ira Progoff, *The Practice of Process Meditation*, Dialogue House Library, N.Y. Scheduled for publication, 1979.

*the Cathedral* the opening of the first meditation is a quotation from the Chinese sage, Lao Tse, "Muddy water, let stand, becomes clear." In the context of Process Meditation the waters correspond to the quality of consciousness within a person. The multiplication of activities and involvements in outer life brings about the muddying of the waters. Conflicts and confusions, the petty and grand turmoils of human existence fill the waters of the mind with a jumble of thoughts and emotions that becloud the consciousness.

It was the accumulation of activities that brought about the muddying of the waters; and it is its opposite, the quieting of the activity, that will return the water to its condition of clarity. "Muddy water, let stand, becomes clear." In *The Well and the Cathedral* our method is to sit in stillness and let the movement of consciousness within us come to rest so that the cycle of inner experience can reestablish itself and renew itself. We do the equivalent in *The White Robed Monk,* establishing a stillness and moving inward within that atmosphere. The cyclical principle is the same, but the style of the symbolism is different.

In *The Well and the Cathedral* we move through the full cycle of inward experience using as our vehicle a set of natural symbols. They are basic, elemental symbols, and this is indicated by the fact that they have appeared in many forms throughout the ages. The image of the well as a representation of spiritual contact is found in the earliest religious writings, not only in the experiences of Jacob in Old Testament days but in the Gilgamesh Epic and in various, more primitive-type stories as well. It is a symbol, but the well also serves as a metaphor that is suggestive of a movement taking place within the person. It represents the process of moving inward into depth. In this sense it is an image that carries its own inherent movement and energies. The image itself is descriptive and suggests the movement of energies into deeper than surface levels. A person, therefore, can recognize and enter into the nature of the process that is represented by the conception of "entering the well". A specific personal experience is not needed because the image itself, as an "elemental symbol", indicates by its very being the nature of the subjective activity that is to take place.*

This is true of the entire sequence of exercises that comprise the method of meditation presented in *The Well and the Cathedral.* Each of the exercises is carried by symbols that are descriptive of their own inner process and are natural to the psyche. They therefore can be entered into and

* See Ira Progoff, *The Symbolic and the Real,* McGraw Hill, N.Y., 1963, Chapter III for a discussion of elemental symbols.

implemented without a personal symbolic experience. That is why *The Well and the Cathedral* is able to serve as a symbolically neutral guide for working in each of the phases of the basic cycle of meditative experience.

*The White Robed Monk* also takes us step by step through this cycle of meditation, but its vehicle is a specific set of symbols that have been personally experienced. Some readers will find that these symbols are congenial to their own experiences, and thus they will be able easily to enter them and work with them, letting them unfold. Others may find that while they do not connect directly with the specific imagery in the meditations, they do feel connected to the atmosphere that is formed around and beyond the symbols. This atmosphere in which the experiences take place seems to have a power that is not limited by the particular symbols that are presented within it. It contains them and is effective within its own terms. Because of this, when a person is drawn into the atmosphere of symbolic experience by an entrance meditation, the way is opened for them to have many new experiences of their own. These experiences may be carried by the symbolism of the meditations or by any other symbols. They may be symbols deliberately chosen for the experience, or they may be totally unexpected symbols stimulated by the depth and spontaneity of the meditative exercise.

The main difference between the two meditative texts is that in *The Well and the Cathedral* we move through the full cycle of meditation using as our vehicle a set of neutrally descriptive metaphors. We move with them through each of the steps in the meditative cycle from the initial state of confusion to the settling into quietness, then to the inward exploration followed by the deepened awareness leading to new contact with further sources of inspiration and eventually a new energy and activity. *The White Robed Monk* takes us through the same cycle, but it does so by means of a symbolism that is more specific. It proceeds within a particular context of individual experience, but it reaches beyond the individual to a universality of contact. Comparing the way of *The Well and the Cathedral* with the way of *The White Robed Monk* leads us to recognize the fact that by whichever road we travel, whether the general or the particular, we eventually reach the universal if we persist and go deep enough. And we see also that the way of that deepening follows the single sequence of steps that comprise the basic cycle of inner experience. It is the cycle that we perceive to be at the heart both of the process of meditation and the process of creativity.

The first phase of the cycle is the establishment of an inner quiet, the stilling of the Self. In *The Well and the Cathedral* it is the settling of the waters, a general image; and in *The White Robed Monk* it comes by specific experiences and practices.*

Each of the eight sections is in fact a small cycle in itself, and each contains its quality of quietness. As the cycle moves on, the dialectical principle within the process of meditation progressively expresses itself. The inner condition moves toward its opposite. The water becomes quiet, and gradually the muddiness settles to the bottom. In the language of *The Well and the Cathedral,* "At the surface it becomes clear," as a quiet lake, and it reflects as a mirror reflects.

The inner experience of a human being parallels this process of nature. Although the circumstances of life may be in turmoil, when a person becomes inwardly still the conflicts and confusions come to rest. It is as though they find a quiet place within the person where they can come together without disturbing other facets of the life. It is the muddiness settling to the bottom. The mind of the person—both the conscious and the unconscious mind, the psyche as a whole—becomes as a quiet lake. Reflections then arise within it like images in quiet water. In the human being, however, these images take the form of thoughts and ideas, visions and hunches,

* See, for example, Sections I and V below.

feelings and understandings, new awarenesses and stimulations to new courses of action in our lives. The quietness established in the person makes it possible for a new imagery of awareness to become available to consciousness. The symbolic experiences that are activated in the time of quietness bring new inspirations and stimulations of thought as well as new energies that arise out of the stillness.

All of this provides the materials for a new surge of activity both inner and outer. When the condition of turmoil has settled into quiet and clarity, there comes a further step, the spontaneous stimulation of new ideas and new projects. Thus we see that the point of the cycle when turmoil has given way to stillness is the turning point of the process. Once the stillness is established, the cycle of experience begins to reverse itself. It moves upward and outward into the realm of activity. New projects, new involvements are drawn to the fore, and soon the energies that had become quiet have generated so much activity that they are jumbled again. Many good productive works are brought about in the course of this phase of the cycle, for it is the resurgence of creativity in a life that had been stalemated. The person comes alive again with thoughts of new possibilities, plans, and projections for the future.

A primary effect of this activity is that it changes the inner atmosphere once again. Now the condition of muddiness has returned. It is now necessary for us to move through the steps of the meditative process once again in order that our renewed confusion can balance itself and that we can reestablish a condition of quiet within ourselves. We have gone full cycle, and we move through this cycle again and again as the process of meditation fits together with, supplies and balances the process of our life experience.

We see here that the process of meditation and the process of life experience are two sides of a single coin. They are in fact the two opposite and complementary aspects of a single process. Taken together, they comprise the continuity of the individual human existence, moving back and forth from an interior to an exterior emphasis. When the outer involvements of life multiply with projects and concerns, we are brought into a state of inner muddiness. Then we have to take the steps that lead to quietness. In the course of our doing this, the focus of our attention is turned to our interior condition.

As we work inwardly to reestablish a stillness of being, we are also setting in motion the dynamic principle that is at the heart of the meditative cycle. As it carries the process back from the excitements of outer activity into the phase of inner stillness, it shifts the movement of energy from an outer to an inner direction. It generates a momentum in the depths of the person, a stirring of energy that activates the contents of the unconscious levels of the psyche.

This has two main effects. One is that, as it stimulates latent knowledge at the depth level, it awakens new ideas for action. It thus renews and often increases the movement of energies going back outward into the world, into whatever projects will give outer expression to the newly awakened inner resources.

The second is that the time of stillness becomes a time of deepened spiritual discovery. The settling into quietness allows outer distractions to drop to one side while symbols and doctrines with which one had not been consciously concerned become the base of fresh inner experiences. Often these are spontaneous and unexpected experiences. They come into consciousness from the place of silence, carrying unpremeditated insights into the mysteries of human existence and our personal life. They are carriers of messages from the depth of the Self, messages from a source more profound than the conscious or intellectual mind. Because their symbolism is unclear, it is often difficult to decipher what the precise meaning of the messages is. But the contents of these experiences, coming in the form of image and symbol, are like reflections from the depth of quiet waters. Some may be merely interesting or titillating; but others may be a most valuable resource in the personal quest for a larger truth.

A main purpose of entrance meditations like *The White Robed Monk* is to give us access to this more-than-personal source of cognition. The quest for meaning in personal life requires a method of gaining entry to the depths of the Self, for that is where the sources and symbols of meaning can be reached. Our entrance meditation enables us to take the first essential steps.

We begin by quieting, by establishing a condition of stillness. As you are preparing to use the text of *The White Robed Monk,* start by sitting in quietness. Just to sit, apparently doing nothing, is a very constructive act toward the meditative goal of reaching the sources of meaning in life.

The next important step is breathing. Not any special or complicated calisthenic of breathing, but simply breathing. We breathe in our accustomed way, the way that feels natural and comfortable to us. But now, as we are sitting in stillness, we breathe a little more slowly than we ordinarily would. First we establish the rhythm that feels right to us, and then we try to continue in a regular and balanced way maintaining the rhythm.

Sustaining the breathing in a regular and comfortable rhythm is a most important step in beginning the process of meditation. As we proceed and become more accustomed to it, we let ourselves go a little slower and a little slower. Bit by bit in our time of quietness, our breathing slows its pace. As it does so, our entire being, our thinking, our feeling, the tempo of our consciousness and our life, slows its pace. It is a time when the muddiness of our existence can settle into stillness and begin to clarify itself. The first section in *The White Robed Monk* is devoted to this quieting, to the sitting and the breathing, and especially to beginning the process by which our consciousness reaches beyond the concerns of our personal existence.

Having begun to breathe in stillness, we now read the text of the entrance meditation. After we have read the text to ourselves in full so that we have perspective of the whole, we return to move through it slowly, a section at a time. We may then feel that our meditation will be helped by hearing sections of *The White Robed Monk* read to us so that we will be altogether free to proceed with closed eyes in exploring inwardly and then recording our experiences. That is the purpose of the cassette reading of *The White Robed Monk;* it can be used to supplement the written word.*

* The cassette recording of Ira Progoff reading the complete text of *The White Robed Monk* is available from Dialogue House Library, 80 East 11 Street, N.Y., N.Y. 10003.

It is good, however, to carry through the main part of our meditative work with the written text open before us. That will help in our understanding of the work. And it also is the way that we accumulate practice in moving back and forth from the outer world to the inner world and back again, and from the world of reading with open eyes to the world of inner perceptions with closed eyes, returning from time to time to record briefly (often with only slightly open eyes) the experiences that have come to us; and then going back and forth as a courier between the inner and outer realms. It is this movement that makes our meditation a way of mediating between the two complementary dimensions of life. Meditation as mediation is a work of inner communication, making the depths of consciousness accessible to our outer lives, and mutually translating the needs and the meanings of each to the other. With practice, this capacity of inner communication makes an important contribution to the wholeness of the person.

In working with the text of *The White Robed Monk* it is best to proceed slowly, one section at a time, allowing ample time for silence after each unit of meditation. Each section closes with the repeated phrase, "In the Silence . . . In the Silence." This is the cue for each of us to move into our own silence. Eyes closed, we turn our attention inward. We are looking inward, but we are not looking merely for things that can be seen. We are looking inwardly for sounds and words, for symbols and intuitions, for direct knowings and sensations of every kind that may come to us when our attention is turned to the large Twilight realm of Self that lies between unconscious sleep and waking consciousness.* In this state we do not seek any particular type of perception. We do not preconceive what our experience is to be, and especially we do not seek to direct it along any predetermined channel.

When we go into our silence and move into the Twilight range of experience, we are truly exploring, looking for information and guidance from a quality of consciousness within us other than the thoughts of our personal mind. Therefore we try to avoid intruding our expectations and ideas as to what our experience "should" or will be. And in particular, we try to refrain from intruding our desires or our willful directions as to what we "want" our experience to be. We are seeking to learn to draw new awarenesses from the transpersonal wisdom of life that is carried in the depths within us beyond our egos. Therefore

* For discussions of the Twilight area of human experience as expressed in Twilight Imaging and other related aspects of the *Intensive Journal* method, see Ira Progoff, *At a Journal Workshop,* Chapter 6, pp. 77ff. Dialogue House Library, 1975.

we let it come as it comes, while we remain altogether open and receptive.

We are observers of whatever is taking place within us as we sit in silence with our eyes closed and our attention turned inward. What we observe may be visual images that we see, words spoken, themes of music that we hear, sensations within our body, direct intuitive knowings. Whatever its form, as we perceive it we take cognizance of it. We do not judge it, but we recognize it. Neutrally, non-judgmentally, we accept its existence. We accept each perception on the twilight level as it is, as a fact of our inner process and of our observation. We take note of it and we record it without evaluation.

Our experiences on the twilight level are of many kinds and of all grades of significance. Some of our perceptions are casual and transient, as changing and as fleeting as though they were created by an interior kaleidoscope. Others are profound and lasting with a personal, and often a more-than-personal message. Sometimes they signal their larger importance with mysterious themes of symbolism, or with strikingly dramatic scenarios acted out on the twilight level. At other times, although the imagery is impressively dramatic, even awesomely symbolic, its actual importance for our lives is meagre. And then we may find that some small image that we almost overlooked because it seemed inconsequential is the bearer of a most meaningful message we would not want to miss.

It is very difficult to evaluate at the moment of its happening the eventual significance of an experience that comes to us on the twilight level. The emotional intensity, or lack of it, at the moment of its occurrence, can be a very misleading sign easily misjudged. We have to be wary of analyzing our twilight experiences—whether they derive from dreams, imaging, or meditation—lest we read into them some current theory of symbol interpretation. If we impose upon them an intellectual concept that is external to our inner process, however logically self-evident the theory may seem to us at the time, we are in danger of breaking our inner connection with our own depths. We may draw ourselves off the path of our organic process, placing ourselves on someone else's theoretical path, and thus confuse our natural unfoldment. Then it is no longer possible for our twilight experiences to communicate their message to us, for we have separated ourselves from the inner wisdom that is our best resource.

In the course of my practice I have evolved certain guidelines as a protection to make sure that we do not inadvertently separate ourselves from the inner principle of our lives. These have been built into the *Intensive Journal* program.

It is first necessary to avoid judging, analyzing or interpreting whatever twilight experiences come to us. We wish to build an inner momentum, and so we try to avoid the self-consciousness that would inhibit its movement. We proceed then upon the principle that none of the multiplicity of images, symbols and experiences that come to us on the twilight level is to be considered to be in its final or ultimate form. All are in process or, at least, are part of a larger process that contains them. And the most important aspect of this process is that it is in movement in the depth of us, that it has a purpose, and that its destination is not disclosed in advance. Our task is to enable that destination—which is the goal and meaning of each individual destiny—to be reached without being sidetracked by undue confusion and frustration. This is the key to the way we work with the twilight experiences that come to us in our entrance meditations.

The principle that all our inner experiences are moving toward the goal of a further development gives us good reason for not judging them, neither critically nor affirmatively, but being neutral toward their present condition. Whatever form they are in now, since they are moving toward something further, we know that they will have a different form in a little while. It thus makes sense to draw no premature conclusions regarding the images and thoughts that come to us, but to go along with them and to help them toward the goal they are seeking, at least until we have some specific indication of what they may possibly become.

In this perspective we may often perceive small images upon the twilight level that seem only to be passing through us and to have no importance in themselves. As we give them space and freedom for inner movement, however, we find unexpectedly that they have combined with other images that were insignificant by themselves. Together they have formed a new constellation of imagery, a new molecule of imagery with an expanded structure, a content and meaning that was not there before. In its new form the image that seemed valueless before is now the carrier of a new awareness, a new realization, an inspiration for a poem, a painting, the next step in a relationship or a project for work.

Similarly, we find that we have many small, seemingly insignificant thoughts, transient thoughts flitting through our minds. Since we judge them to be of no value, we repress them and try to stop thinking them so that we can get on with other things. But after a while we discover that those passing thoughts which we were not able to control and which we tried to repress have combined with other thoughts on their own. They did this without our guidance and without our approval. They have formed new molecules of thought, new combinations with expanded content, and these give us insight and understanding we did not have before. These new awarenesses did not come through our conscious efforts, but by the energy and the seeking that lay inherent within the thoughts and the images themselves. It is an instance of our thoughts thinking us, our symbols imaging us, and moving through us toward a goal they know better than we. This is a depth phenomenon known to wise men of the past, ancient and modern, men like Meister Eckhart and William James, Albert Einstein and Carl Jung. And we are now rediscovering it for purposes of creativity and spiritual renewal in our time

Understanding what is involved in this process gives us a principle that we can follow individually as we each work in our private spiritual process. When we become quiet we have many bits of thought and imagery that appear spontaneously and fleetingly to us as in a kaleidoscopic movement within our minds. When we perceive them they seem to be of no consequence, and so we often pass them by. But when we realize that they are moving actively toward a goal of meaning within us and that they are seeking to combine with other thoughts and images within us in order to shape new messages and projects for our life, we realize that it is decidedly to our advantage to pay attention to these varied perceptions and to help them fulfill themselves. But how? When we perceive them in their transient state they seem to be insignificant, at least when viewed by themselves. But later on, when they have the opportunity to come together with other thoughts and images to form new composites, we can recognize the inner direction in their movement. We are then able to see what they were trying to become.

For the inner work of spiritual and creative development we require a means of gathering these varied twilight experiences so that their goals and the patterns they are seeking to form can disclose themselves; and so that we do not cut them off prematurely.

A major problem in doing this comes from the fact that these experiences are elusive, fleeting, difficult to hold and examine. Their movement and their changes are so rapid, both in their content as thoughts and their symbolism as images, that we can seldom hold them together long enough to see their content and determine their meaning. In some ways these experiences are like sounds of music, songs spontaneously sung in the quiet of the night. They appear in us, and then they are gone. But if they are permanently gone, undescribed and unremembered, we lose our chance to receive the message they would eventually have for us. That is why it is important for us to record the experiences that come to us in the silences of these meditations.

On the left hand page of this edition is space for our *Meditation Log* entries. Here we record what takes place within us as we explore and experience on the twilight level in the course of our entrance meditations. In what we write here we make no interpretations, nor do we elaborate or explain. We simply describe, briefly and directly, the elusive and subjective perceptions, images and emotions that arise in us in the course of our meditations. And then we move on. It is important also that we record the date of each entry. That will be a valuable piece of information for us when we return to the Meditation Log at a later time.

If you are already working with the *Intensive Journal* process you may wish to record your experiences directly in the *Intensive Journal* workbook that you are using. That will save a step. But a number of persons have told me that they feel they have benefited by using the Meditation Log pages in the companion edition of *The Well and the Cathedral*. They have used the Meditation Log in the printed volume as a means of retaining the spontaneous experiences that came to them while they were working with the text, then copying their entries into the larger Meditation Log section in their *Intensive Journal* workbook. And it is apparently a common experience to find that in the course of copying the entries to transfer them from one book to the other a great deal more is stimulated. Additional experiences are evoked. The recording and transcription of our inner experiences thus become an integral part of the progressive extension of consciousness that is the goal of our Entrance Meditation work.

Those who are already working in the *Intensive Journal* program are familiar with the varied measures available to us for drawing our Meditation Log entries into an expanding spiritual process. They know that in the context of the *Intensive Journal* work the Meditation Log is not merely a passive recording instrument like a diary, but that it serves an active, energy-building function. After collecting the raw material of our inner lives, the Meditation Log selectively feeds the data into the appropriate sections of the *Intensive Journal* workbook. Here this material combines with other relevant images and thoughts recorded in other sections, and together they may move through a varied combination of exercises. All of these are active, psyche-evoking exercises that build energy and movement and generate new inner experiences. In the course of these exercises and experiences the varied beliefs, the religious concerns, and a person's intimations and wonderings about meaning in life are often stimulated so that they can be explored and amplified in a progressive, open-minded reaching toward truth.

In this phase of the work we are finally able to draw upon the full range of possibilities that the *Intensive Journal* method makes available to us. After using the basic *Intensive Journal* techniques to set the perspective of our life history and to clarify our personal relationships, we can now proceed to the more-than-personal issues, the large spiritual agenda of Process Meditation. It is this further phase of the meditative discipline that enables us to expand our spiritual awareness with inner experiences that are directly related to the actualities, the goals and meanings, of our everyday life.*

This is the point of transition in our meditative work. Here we take the important step from the fundamental introductory exercises of Entrance Meditation to the broad range of explora-

* The principles and the program of practices for this amplified use of the Meditation Log are described from two points of view, the personal and the spiritual aspects, in the two volumes that are the basic textbooks for the *Intensive Journal* method, *At a Journal Workshop*, and *The Practice of Process Meditation*.

tions and ongoing spiritual involvements that opens to us with the practice of Process Meditation. By means of Entrance Meditation experiences like *The White Robed Monk* we can enter the dimension of spiritual reality where inner experiences and transpersonal awareness can come to us. We record these in our Meditation Log. These collected entries then become the raw spiritual data that serve as base points from which we launch our active inner explorations using the Process Meditation techniques within the *Intensive Journal* method. It is a continuous, progressive, and deepening work. Process Meditation is a personal discipline for extending our inner evolution by giving us ready access to spiritual sources in support of our religious and creative life.

Now, as we turn to work with the text of *The White Robed Monk,* let us review in our mind the steps that we shall follow as we move through the cycle of experience in each of the sections of our Entrance Meditation. We begin by sitting in stillness, then breathing in a regular rhythm. Working with the meditation texts we close our eyes. We let ourselves be drawn into the twilight range of perception. Having gained entry there, we observe everything that presents itself to us. We make no judgments, neither accepting nor rejecting, but we take cognizance of whatever is present. We observe it all, and we record as much as we can in our Meditation Log. As we gather it together, the accumulation of data gradually discloses a direction and a purpose as new thoughts and images take form. We begin to see potentials of truth and new meaning unfolding through our inner experiences. We realize that it is not by directing nor by manipulating ourselves psychologically, but by being open in a disciplined way to the progressive stirrings within ourselves that we come personally into contact with the spiritual nature that is our individual and collective heritage as human beings.

Having said this much, we must understand that meditation in both its phases, as Entrance Meditation and as Process Meditation, is a work that demonstrates itself and proves itself only as we actually do it. Therefore let us begin, sitting in stillness . . .

Letting the Self become still,
Letting the breath become slow,
Letting the thoughts come to rest.

# I

# *Breathing in the Quiet Place*

*Meditation Log* *Date*

1. I am sitting in quietness.
   The winds of my life
   Are blowing around me
   And within me,
   But I am quiet,
   Sitting,
   Breathing,
   Breathing in the quiet place.

2. Breathing in the quiet place,
   My breath is steady
   And slow,
   Moving in
   And out,
   Regular breathing.
   My breath moves at the center
   Regular breathing
   At the center of my Self.

*Meditation Log* *Date*

3. Breathing in the quiet place
Centered
In stillness
The ebb
And flow
Of my breathing
Is a gentle ocean
Moving within me.
My inner being
Lies silent as the sands
While the waves of my life,
The waves of my breathing,
Rise and fall upon it.

4. Centered and still.
Only the breath is moving.
The ocean of my life,
Moving in the soft waves
Of my breathing,
In and out,
Slow,
Regular.
The breath moves at the center,
At the center of the Self.

*Meditation Log* *Date*

5. The breath moves at the center,
As it breathes
I breathe with it
It becomes my breath.
I know it is more than my breath
But it moves within me.
It is my breath
Moving
As the waves of life,
The rhythm of the great universe
Within my Self.

6. The breath moves at the center.
At the center of my Self.
It is my breath
And the breath of life,
The breath of all,
Moving
In and out
In my breathing.
It breathes me
As I breathe it,
The Great Breath
And my breath
Breathing together
In the stillness.

*Meditation Log* *Date*

7. The breath moves at the center.
   It breathes me
   As I breathe it.
   It is one breath,
   The great breath,
   The breath of all
   And my small breath,
   Moving in and out
   As one breath.

8. The great breath of all
   Breathing in me
   As I breathe it.
   It breathes at the center,
   At the center of my Self.
   It breathes me
   As I breathe it.
   We go in and out
   Together
   In the Silence . . . In the Silence.

# II

# *Finding My Way Through Darkness*

*Meditation Log* *Date*

1. Sitting in stillness
Breathing.
Breathing
At the depth of stillness,
Something stirs in me.
It draws me
Out of my stillness.
It stirs in me
And draws me on
To explore what I know not.
I rouse myself and follow it.
I go with it
Not knowing where.

2. The stirring within me
Leads me down dark corridors
Where there is no light.
Not seeing where I am walking,
I walk onwards.
Looking ahead
I see nothing.
There is no end in sight.

3. I wonder at it,
But the stirring within me
Draws me on.
I continue walking,
Following it
Down narrow, winding corridors.
The walls are of stone,
Cold and ancient stones
Leading downward
Into darkness.

4. I walk on
Not knowing where I am walking.
All at once a light before me
A room full of light.
It is a chapel
Underground,
Hidden in the darkness
But filled with light.

*Meditation Log* *Date*

5. In the center of the chapel
Is an altar.
It is flat and round,
The stump of an ancient tree.
No one is at the altar
But a radiance comes from it
Drawing me into the chapel.
I enter
And go directly to the altar.

6. All that walking through darkness,
Walking without knowing where,
Has been leading me here
To the underground chapel,
To the tree
In the midst of the chapel,
The flat, round stump of a tree,
The altar/tree.

*Meditation Log* *Date*

7. Finding my way to the altar/tree
Has been difficult.
Not knowing it was here
I could not seek it.
But walking
Not knowing where,
Seeking
Not knowing what,
I have found my way
Through darkness
To the altar/tree
At the center of the chapel.

8. I am at rest now
At the center of the chapel
Feeling the presence of the altar
As I stand before it,
Reviewing in my mind
The journey of my past.
Finding my way through darkness,
I have come
To the underground chapel,
A quiet place of light
Hidden but present
I know not where.

*Meditation Log* *Date*

9. I feel welcome by the altar/tree.
It is comforting to be here
Reviewing my journey,
Recalling the darkness
In this atmosphere of light.
My heart opens
As I stand before the altar
Considering my life,
Reviewing the past
And wondering at the future.
I place my life upon the altar.
I place my life upon the altar
In the Silence . . . In the Silence.

# III

# *Standing at the Altar / Tree*

*Meditation Log* *Date*

1. I am standing before the altar
Of the underground chapel,
The stump of an ancient tree,
Massive,
The power of ages
Compressed within it.
Ancient,
Alone,
It stands self-contained.

2. The altar/tree
Is centered in itself.
I feel the primeval depths
Of the beginnings of life
Move through the rings
Of the aged wood.
How far back they go,
How present they are.

*Meditation Log* *Date*

3. I feel myself entering
The center of the rings
Of the aged wood.
They quiet me,
They focus me.
I feel myself to be
At the center
Of the circles of time
There in the circles
Of the altar/tree.

4. I feel the movement of time
There in the circles of the tree,
I feel the movement of time
In the center of my Self.
I stand before the altar/tree
Centered in its circles,
Swirling inward
In the rings of time,
Time before time,
Time beyond time.

*Meditation Log* *Date*

5. I go into the swirling circles,
Into the timeless circles
Of the tree of life,
I stand before the ancient remains
Of the tree of life,
The altar/tree
Of the underground chapel.

6. I am standing before it now
Feeling my life.
Feeling my life
With all else that lives
And has ever lived,
There in the rings of time
At the center of the altar/tree.

7. I stand before the altar/tree
Entering its circles,
Moving into it,
Feeling time beyond time
Present now,
Here
In the movement of my life.

*Meditation Log* *Date*

8. Feeling the years of my life
Passing through time,
Feeling the timeless in my life
Present
In this moment.
Feeling the timeless in time,
Knowing it,
Being it . . .
In the Silence . . . In the Silence.

# IV

# *The Silent Work of the Monks*

*Meditation Log* *Date*

1. As I stand in the silence
Before the altar/tree
I become aware
That others are present
In the underground chapel.
I see
Monks in brown robes
Seated on every side.
Their heads are bowed,
They are in silence.

2. The monks do not raise their eyes,
But they know I am here.
They have permitted me to enter.
The warmth of their silence
Enters me
And encourages me
To be with them.

3. I take a place on a bench
Beside the brown robed monks.
Each is intent
Upon his own work.
No one speaks,
But something emanates
From each of the monks.

*Meditation Log* *Date*

4. These emanations
From the monks
Are like sparks,
But not sparks that burn.
They are sparks
That give glistenings of light;
They are warm and bright
But they do not burn.

5. A power
Becomes present in the silence.
It comes from something stirring
In the silence of the monks,
In the silence of the chapel.
The power is carried
By emanations of love
Coming from the monks,
Healing,
Strengthening,
Warming the air around me.

*Meditation Log* *Date*

6. An atmosphere is forming around me.
I move deeper into it,
Absorbed by it,
Drawn into
The silent work of the monks,
Each intent on his own work
And all contributing to all.
Each and all
Silently adding
His stirrings of love
To the energies of everyone.

7. I am sitting
In the warmth of the chapel.
The silent stirrings of love
Move around me.
Carried by my breath,
They enter me.
They move around within me
And become a great warmth,
A great warmth within me
And a great warmth around me.

*Meditation Log* *Date*

8. Drawn inward by my breath,
The atmosphere enters my Self.
It circulates within me,
It moves within me.
Carried by my breath,
The outward atmosphere
Of the chapel
Becomes an inward atmosphere
Within my Self.

9. I am sitting
In the warmth of the chapel
As we each do our inward work,
Working together,
Alone
And together . . .
Sharing the work of the monks
In the Silence . . . In the Silence.

# V

# *Breathing at One with the Monks*

*Meditation Log* *Date*

1. Sitting in the chapel
   Sharing the warmth of the monks,
   Breathing their atmosphere,
   I become quiet
   As they are quiet.

2. From the midst of this quietness
   Stirrings arise within me,
   Stirrings of many kinds.
   I welcome them,
   I take note of these stirrings
   As they come to me
   In the atmosphere of the chapel.

3. Breathing at one with the monks
   Soft stirrings of light
   Arise within me.
   They form a special light
   By which I see
   Inwardly.

*Meditation Log* *Date*

4. In that light
My vision opens.
Doors that were narrow
Now open wide within me,
And I recognize many things
That were strange to me before;
They were distant before
But now they are near,
For I know them from within.

5. My heart opens
And hears
Words and sounds
That have long been waiting
To be heard.
Now I hear them.
Things I cannot see
And words I cannot hear
Melt into me,
And I know them
From within my Self.

*Meditation Log* *Date*

6. The warmth of the monks,
The inward warmth of the chapel
Melts all things into me;
All things become one with me
And I become one with them.
Unity of knowing,
Unity of being,
It is so.

7. The universe opens within me.
Narrow doors of my mind
Are opening wide
Beyond my mind,
Beyond my Self.
I see things,
I recognize truths
By inward stirrings of light.

8. The universe is opening
Within me.
Many levels of knowing
Spread themselves before me
As I sit in the chapel
Breathing at one with the monks,
Breathing at one with the monks . . .
In the Silence . . . In the Silence.

# VI

# *The White Robed Monk with No Face*

*Meditation Log* *Date*

1. Seated in the underground chapel
In the stillness,
Carried by their breathing,
Warmed by their atmosphere,
Each engaged in his inward work,
The monks pause.
They raise their eyes.

2. Another person enters.
He is another monk,
A monk in white robes
And his face has no features.
It is blank
As a mirror is blank,
And clear
As a mirror is clear.
His face has no features
But it shines,
It shines with an effulgent glow.

*Meditation Log* *Date*

3. The monks rise as he enters.
As he walks through the chapel
They begin to chant:
Kyrie Eleison,
Kyrie Eleison.
The white robed monk walks
Up a diagonal aisle to the altar,
Then around it,
Down another aisle
And around the chapel,
Then up another aisle
Toward the altar
And around it.
He does this many times.

*Meditation Log* *Date*

4. All the while the monks are chanting:
Kyrie Eleison,
Kyrie Eleison.
Chanting,
Chanting in mellow tones
And in a regular rhythm.
The chanting in the chapel
Fills the atmosphere,
Kyrie Eleison,
I hear it echo around me.
It continues to echo
Within me.
Kyrie Eleison.

5. The monk in white robes
Now goes to the altar.
He stands before it
In perfect stillness.
The chanting has ended,
Its echo is fading away.
He stands in silence,
Straight in his bearing.
His head is erect
But his face has no features.
It is clear
As a mirror is clear.

*Meditation Log* *Date*

6. I gaze into the face
Of the white robed monk.
It is a faceless face
And it reflects endlessly,
Endlessly.
The monks look deep,
Deep into the mirror
Of the clear, faceless face
Of the white robed monk.
I look with them.

7. Intently gazing
Deep into the mirror
Of the faceless face
Of the white robed monk,
I see things reflected there.
But it is not physical things
That I see.
I see my own face
Reflected there,
But it is not my physical face
That I see.
I am seeing my inner face,
I am seeing unseeable things.

*Meditation Log* *Date*

8. I see thoughts
One after another,
Fears and wishes,
Wonderings
and worryings,
Hopes and pleasures,
Doubts,
Courage and despair,
Clarity mixed with confusion.
Unseeable shapes and forms I see,
Looking deep into the faceless face
Of the white robed monk.

9. Everything is there,
It is a mirror of the soul.
The faceless face
Of the white robed monk
Is a mirror of the soul.
Each of the monks
Looks deep into it,
Endlessly,
Endlessly deep.
I also see
Reflections of my life
And more than my life
In the mirror of the soul.

*Meditation Log* *Date*

10. The monks and I
Together
Looking
Into the faceless face
Of the white robed monk.
Looking,
Finding,
Seeing the unseeable
In the mirror of the soul.
Together
Looking,
Each of us
Looking . . .
In the Silence . . . In the Silence.

# VII

# *The Words of the White Robed Monk*

*Meditation Log* *Date*

1. The monks are resting now.
With eyes closed
They sit in quietness,
Resting
From what they have seen,
And waiting
For the white robed monk
To speak.

2. There is silence
And expectancy.
The monk in white robes
Is about to speak.
The monks are listening,
And from their intensity I can tell
That each monk is hearing words
With great meaning for him.

3. The white robed monk
Is already speaking.
But I hear nothing.
Why do I alone hear nothing?
I become agitated inside,
A storm is brewing within me.
But I let it be.
It settles
And I become quiet again.

*Meditation Log* *Date*

4. Presently
In my quietness
I too hear words spoken
By the white robed monk.
The words seem to come
Out of the glow in his face.
I do not hear them
As words are heard;
They are not heard by the ear,
But they are heard inwardly.
They are heard
Within
Each of the monks
And within me.
Different words
Are heard
By each of us.

*Meditation Log* *Date*

5. My eyes are closed
And I am listening intently
To hear the words
Spoken by the white robed monk.
The monks and I
Are listening,
Inwardly hearing
The words of the white robed monk,
The words of the white robed monk.

6. As we listen
Each hears his own message
In his own silence,
Each hears the message
That speaks to his life,
That speaks to his soul,
Hearing with an interior ear
The message
Spoken by the white robed monk.
He speaks to each of us
Personally.
He speaks to me
Of my life
And he speaks of the life
Of everyone.

*Meditation Log* *Date*

7. I listen as he speaks.
Let us listen together,
Each of us listening
In our own stillness,
Hearing our own message.
Let us listen together,
Each of us alone
And together as one,
Listening . . .
In the Silence . . . In the Silence.

# VIII

## *In The Chapel of The Self*

*Meditation Log* *Date*

1. Standing at the altar/tree
The white robed monk is speaking.
No words are heard by the ear
But we recognize words
Within ourselves.
We hear them inwardly
Each in our own way,
Hearing the words
That each soul draws
From the soul
Of the white robed monk.

2. The words come.
We hear them spoken
Within us
And we write them.
While we write
More words come to us
Than we were aware we heard.
Thus the white robed monk
Multiplies the teaching
That he gives us
While we sit in silence
Listening.

*Meditation Log* *Date*

3. As he speaks from the altar/tree
It is within ourselves
That we recognize him
And hear him
And feel his presence.
The white robed monk comes to us
In the midst of the silence
Of the chapel,
In the midst of the silence
Of the Self
Wherever we are.
Having recognized him once,
We may recognize him always.

4. The white robed monk is present,
Present
In the chapel of the Self,
Speaking there
And speaking also
In the midst of the world.
He speaks to us
And for us
In the midst of the noise
And the turmoil
Of the world
Wherever we create
An atom of silence
Within our life.

5. An atom of silence
Wherever it can be formed
Provides a center
In the midst of turmoil,
A quiet place of peace,
A secret chapel
Where the white robed monk
Can be present
And speak.

6. Wherever we are,
   Whatever is happening,
   The white robed monk speaks to us
   In our secret chapel.
   In our atom of silence
   He is present
   Reflecting our lives
   In his infinite face,
   The mirror of the soul,
   Giving a message
   That we alone can see,
   That we alone
   Can understand.

7. The white robed monk comes to us
   In the midst of our turmoil
   Wherever we are
   As we become quiet
   And form
   An atom of silence
   At the center of the Self.

*Meditation Log* *Date*

8. In that atom of silence
We enter
The hidden chapel
Where the white robed monk
Is present.
In that inward chapel
The loving warmth of the monks
Sustains us
While we listen,
Each hearing
Our own true word.

9. We are there now
In the chapel of the Self
Feeling the warmth of the monks,
Breathing at one with the monks,
Sharing the work of the monks
And listening with them
As the white robed monk speaks,
Saying a different word
To each of us.
We are listening together,
Listening
In the Silence . . . In the Silence.